A Mother's Love

Like flowers, children grow and bloom with loving care. This design by Diane Brakefield captures the beauty of a mother's sweet love. What a wonderful gift it will make on Mother's Day or any time of year!

HOW TO READ THE CHART

Each section of the chart is made up of a key and a gridded design on which each square represents a stitch. The symbols in the key tell which floss color to use for each stitch in the chart. The following headings and symbols are given:

X — Cross Stitch
DMC — DMC color number
1/4**X** — Quarter Stitch
1/2**X** — Half Cross Stitch
B'ST — Backstitch

A square filled with a color and a symbol should be worked as a Cross Stitch.

A triangle should be worked as a Quarter Stitch.

A straight line should be worked as a Backstitch.

A large dot listed near the end of the key should be worked as a French Knot or it may indicate bead placement.

Sometimes the symbol for a **Cross Stitch** may be partially covered or completely absent when a **Backstitch** crosses the square. Refer to the background color to determine the floss color.

I0879196

HOW TO STITCH

Always work Cross Stitches and Quarter Stitches first and then add the Backstitch and French Knots.

How to Determine the Finished Size

The finished size of your design will depend on the thread count per inch of the fabric being used. To determine the finished size of the design on different fabrics, divide the number of squares (stitches) in the width of the charted design by the thread count of the fabric. For example, a charted design with a width of 80 squares worked on 14 count Aida will yield a design 5 3/4" wide. Repeat for the number of squares (stitches) in the height of the charted design. *(**Note:** To work over two fabric threads, divide the number of squares by one-half the thread count.)* Then add the amount of background you want plus a generous amount for finishing, usually 3"-4" on all sides if the design will be framed.

Preparing Fabric

Being sure to allow plenty of margin, cut the fabric to the desired size and overcast the raw edges. It is better to waste a little fabric than to come up short after many hours of stitching.

Working with Floss

To ensure smoother stitches, separate floss strands and realign them before threading the needle. Keep stitching tension consistent. Begin and end floss by running under several stitches on the back; never tie knots.

LEISURE ARTS, INC. • Maumelle, Arkansas

HOW TO STITCH *(Continued)*

Where to Start

The horizontal and vertical centers of the charted design are shown by arrows. You may start at any point on the charted design, but be sure the design will be centered on the fabric. Locate the center of the fabric by folding it in half, top to bottom and again left to right. On the charted design, count the number of squares (stitches) from the center of the chart to where you wish to start. Then, from the fabric's center, find your starting point by counting out the number of fabric threads (stitches). (To work over two fabric threads, count out twice the number of fabric threads.)

To add support to stitches when stitching over two fabric threads, it is important that the first Cross Stitch is placed on the fabric with stitch 1-2 beginning and ending where a vertical fabric thread crosses over a horizontal fabric thread *(Fig. 1)*. When the first stitch is in the correct position, the entire design will be placed properly, with vertical fabric threads supporting each stitch.

Fig. 1

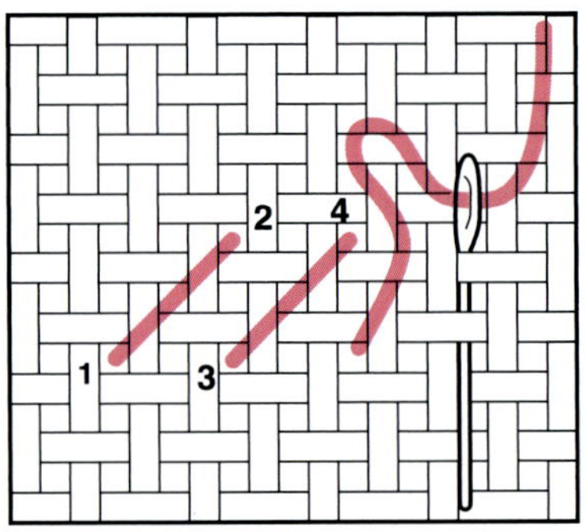

STITCH DIAGRAMS

When stitching, bring the threaded needle up at 1 and all odd numbers and down at 2 and all even numbers.

Cross Stitch (X): For horizontal rows, work stitches in two journeys *(Fig. 2)*. For vertical rows, complete each stitch as shown *(Fig. 3)*. When working over two fabric threads, work Cross Stitch as shown in **Fig. 4.**

Fig. 2

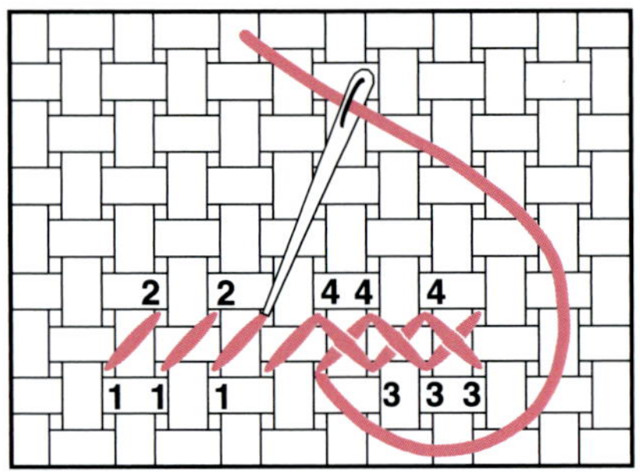

Fig. 3

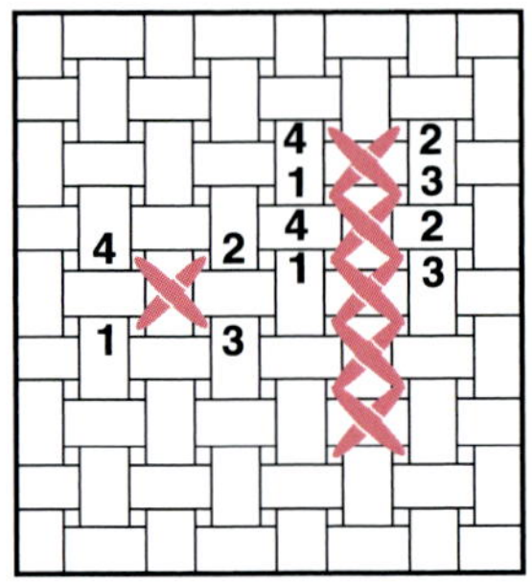

Fig. 4

Quarter Stitch (¼X): Come up at 1, and then split the fabric thread to go down at 2 *(Fig. 5)*. Fig. 6 shows the technique for the Quarter Stitch when working over two fabric threads.

Fig. 5

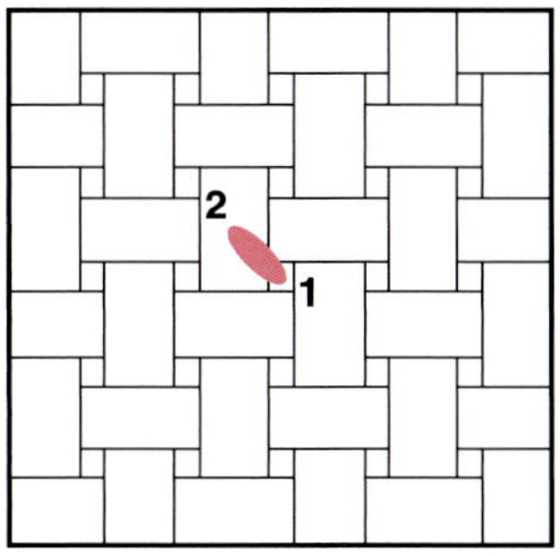

Fig. 6

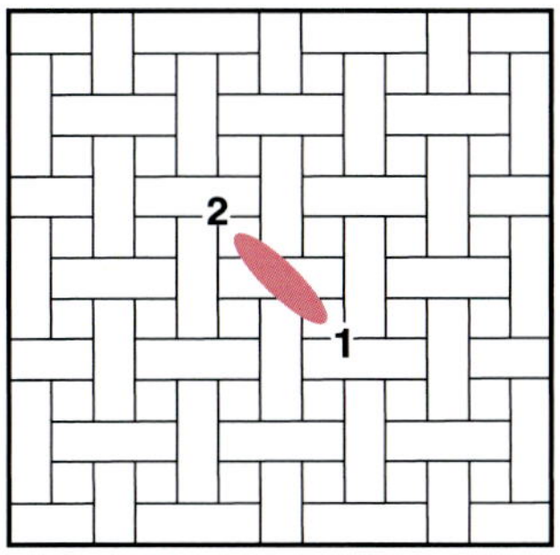

Backstitch (B'ST): For outlines and details, Backstitch should be worked after the design has been completed *(Fig. 7)*. When working over two fabric threads, work the Backstitch as shown in Fig. 8.

Fig. 7

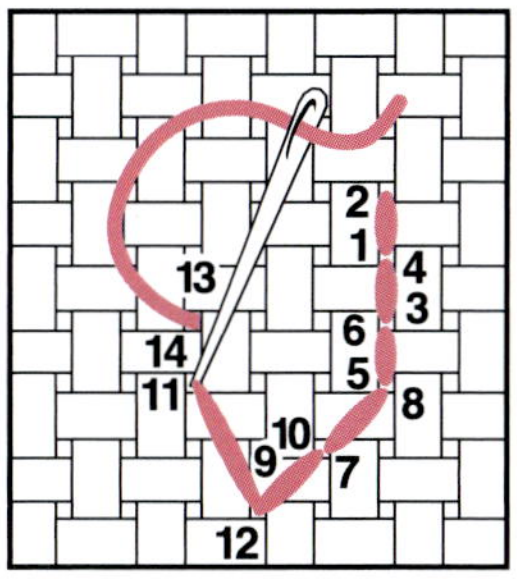

Fig. 8

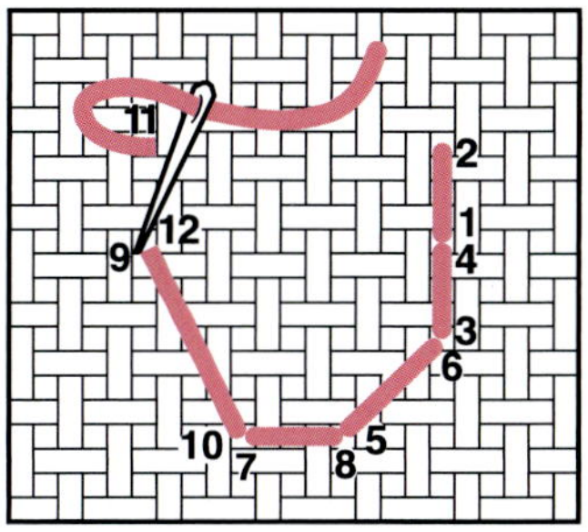

French Knot: Bring the needle up at 1. Wrap the floss once around the needle. Insert the needle at 2, tighten the knot, and pull the needle through the fabric, holding the floss until it must be released *(Fig. 9)*. For a larger knot, use more floss strands and wrap only once.

Fig. 9

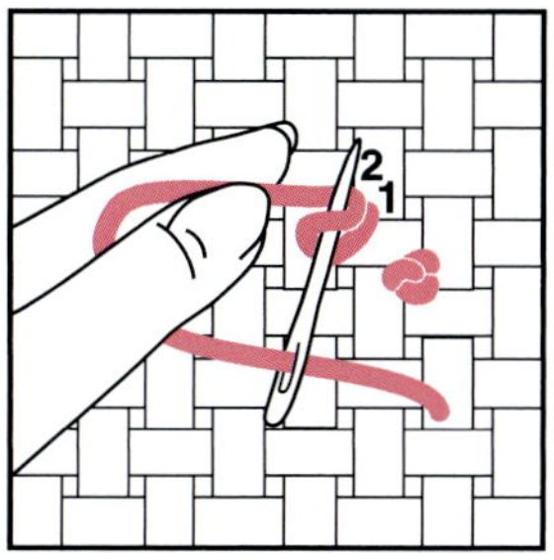

THE SEWING METHOD

Cross Stitches should be worked over two fabric threads on linen fabric. When working over two fabric threads, you may choose to use the sewing method instead of the stab method.

To use the sewing method, keep your stitching hand on the right side of the fabric (instead of stabbing the fabric with the needle and taking your stitching hand to the back of the fabric to pick up the needle). With the sewing method, you take the needle down and up with one stroke instead of two.

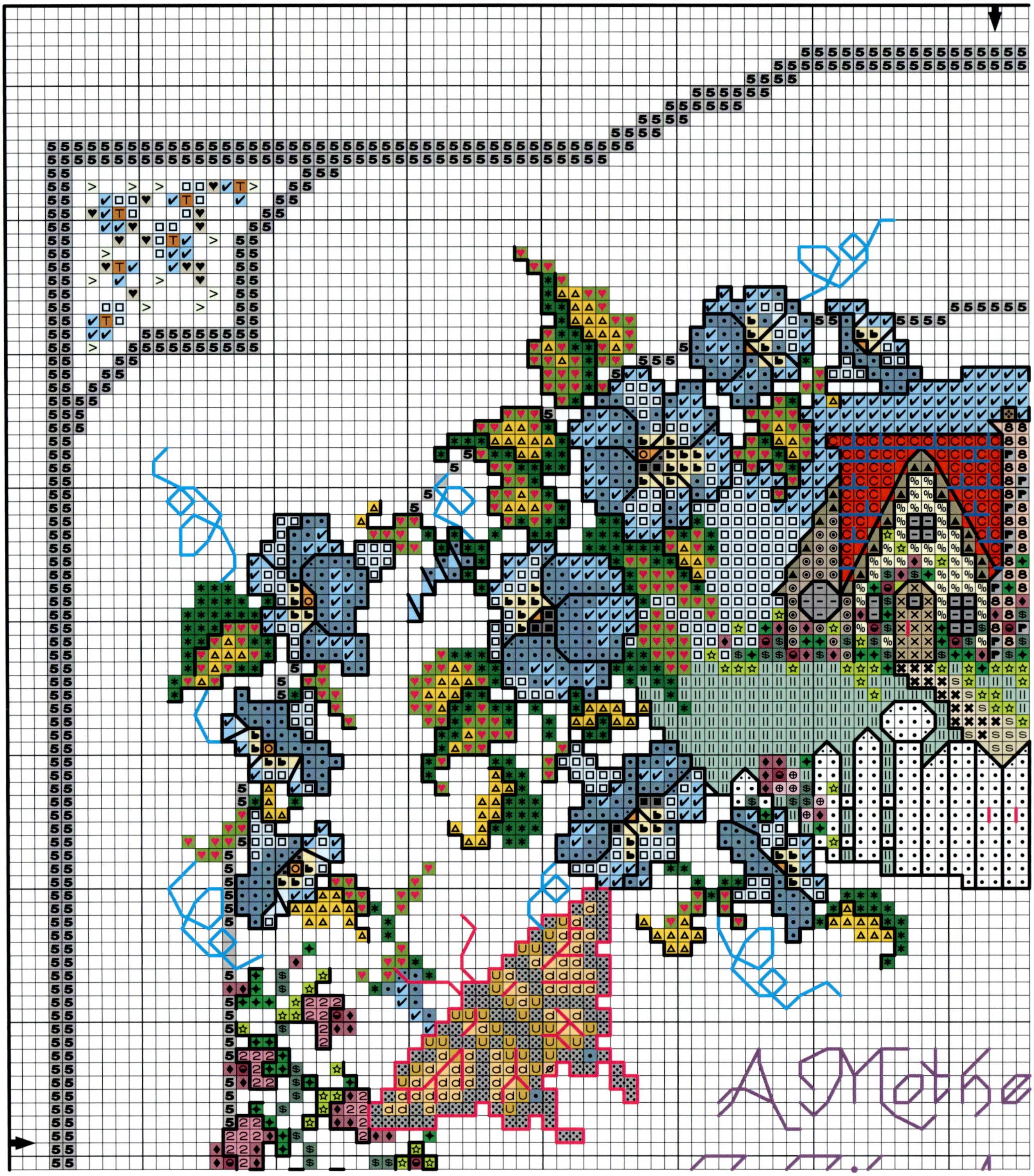

A Mother's Love

The design was stitched over 2 fabric threads on a 17" x 18" piece of 32 count Antique White Belfast Linen (design size $8^{7}/_{8}$" x $10^{1}/_{4}$"). Two strands of floss were used for Cross Stitches and Quarter Stitches and 1 strand for Backstitches and French Knots. The design was custom framed.

X	DMC	¼ X	B'ST
•	blanc	•	
Σ	211		
⁘	310	◪	/
×	318		
*	320		
★	327	◪	
+	340		
	367		/
♥	368		
△	369		

X	DMC	¼ X	B'ST
	413		/
■	414	◪	/
−	415	◪	
⁘	436	◪	
$	500	◪	/
✦	502		
☆	503	◪	
ll	504	◪	
□	550	◪	
✪	553		

X	DMC	¼ X
◇	554	
▲	646	◪
4	647	
C	648	◪
	704	◪
⁘	718	
ø	722	
T	725	◪
O	726	◪
d	727	

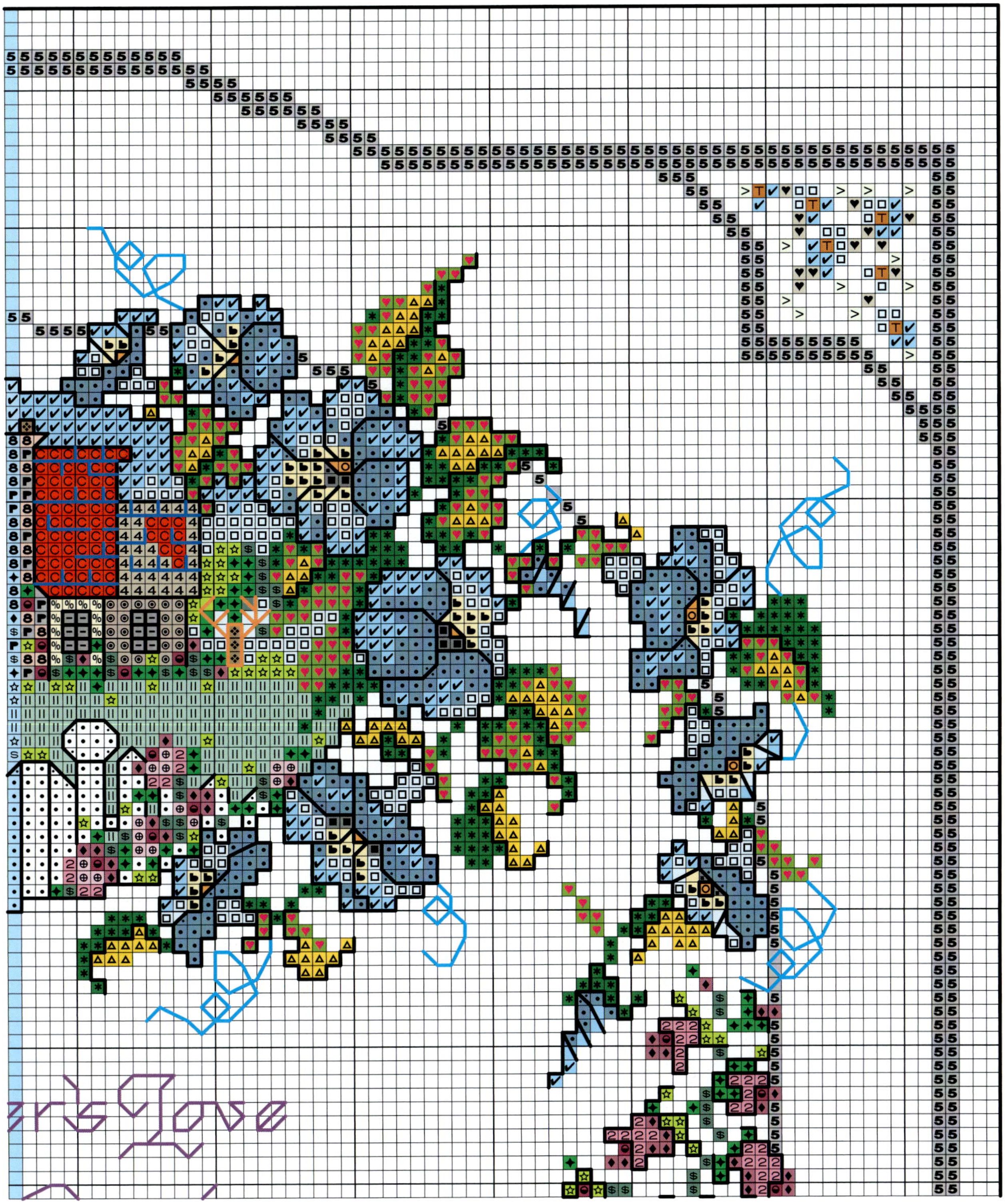

X	DMC	1/4 X	B'ST
%	746		
5	762		
>	772		
□	775		
✔	800		
X	840		
S	841		
V	991		
❖	3031		
◉	3047		
◣	3078		
♥	3347		
H	3608		
=	3609		
⊖	3685		
◆	3687		
2	3688		
⊕	3689		
▼	3746		
/	3747		
•	3755		
8	3773		
P	3778		
✖	3782		
♡	3816		
U	3821		
•	500 French Knot		
	Blue area indicates last row of previous section of design.		

Stitch Count (141w x 164h)	
14 count	$10^1/_8$" x $11^3/_4$"
16 count	$8^7/_8$" x $10^1/_4$"
18 count	$7^7/_8$" x $9^1/_8$"

X	DMC	1/4 X	B'ST
•	blanc	■	
Σ	211		
⁘	310	■	■
×	318		
✱	320		
★	327	■	
+	340		
	367		■
♥	368		
△	369		
	413		■
■	414	■	■
-	415	■	
⁘	436	■	
$	500	■	■
✦	502		
☆	503	■	
‖	504	■	
▣	550	■	
✪	553		
◇	554		
▲	646	■	
4	647		
C	648	■	
	704	■	
⁘	718		
ø	722		
T	725	■	
O	726	■	
d	727		
%	746	■	
5	762		
>	772		
□	775	■	
✓	800	■	
×	840	■	
S	841	■	
V	991		
❖	3031		■
◎	3047	■	

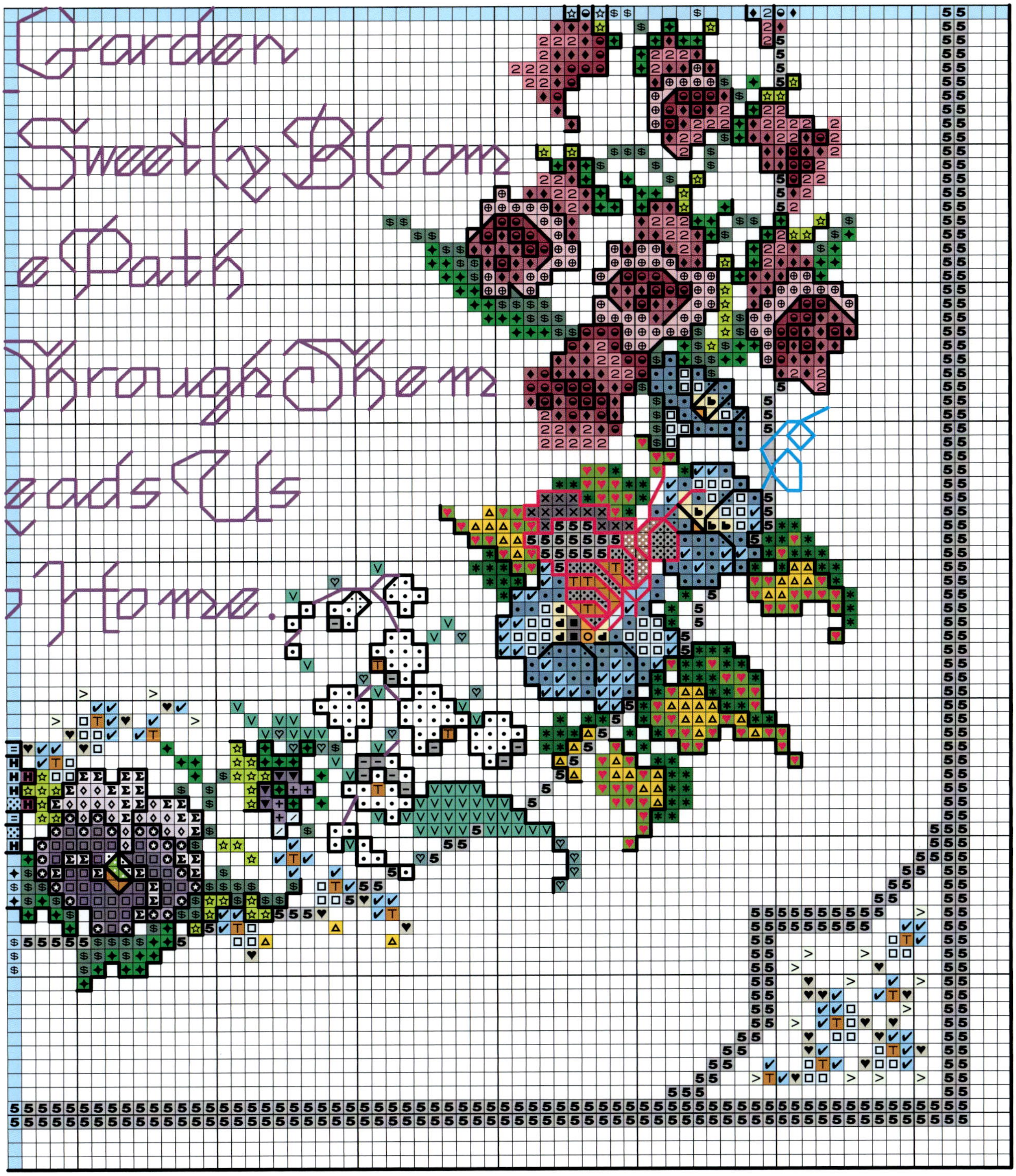

X	DMC	1/4 X
b	3078	✓
♥	3347	
H	3608	
=	3609	
⊖	3685	✓
♦	3687	✓
2	3688	✓
⊕	3689	✓
▼	3746	✓
/	3747	✓
•	3755	✓
8	3773	✓
P	3778	✓
✖	3782	
♡	3816	
U	3821	
•	500 French Knot	
	Blue area indicates last row of previous section of design.	

Show us what you're working on!

Share your project photos with us on social media.
Tag us @leisureartsinc or use #leisurearts

Production Team: Technical Writer – Mary Hutcheson; Editorial Writer – Susan Frantz Wiles; Senior Graphic Artist – Lora Puls; Graphic Artist – Frances Huddleston; Photographer – Ken West .

Made in U.S.A.